THE LITTLE BOOK OF
CHURCHILL

Published by Orange Hippo!
20 Mortimer Street
London W1T 3JW

Disclaimer:

ISBN 978-1-91161-041-0

Editorial: Stella Caldwell, Victoria Godden
Project manager: Russell Porter
Design: Darren Jordan
Production: Jessica Arvidsson

A CIP catalogue for this book is available from the British Library

Printed in Dubai

10 9 8 7 6 5 4 3 2 1

Jacket cover photograph: Dayat Banggai/Shutterstock

THE LITTLE BOOK OF

CHURCHILL

IN HIS OWN WORDS

CONTENTS

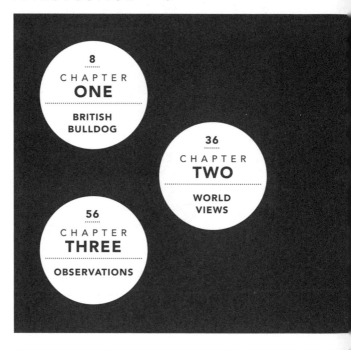

INTRODUCTION

Churchill is rightly remembered as a great wartime leader – the British bulldog who steered the nation through Dunkirk, the Battle of Britain and the Blitz, and rallied the British people to defy Hitler.

But he is also remembered for many other things: his sense of adventure, his larger-than-life personality, his cigars and his famous victory salute. And he is, of course, remembered for his way with words: the fine writing that won him the Nobel Prize for Literature in 1953; his rousing speeches; his barbed putdowns; and his witty asides.

In 1963, President John F. Kennedy captured the essence of Churchill's talent when he wrote, "In the dark days… when Britain stood alone – and most men save Englishmen despaired of England's life – he mobilised the English language and sent it into battle."

Of course, Churchill's mastery of the English language was in evidence long before his "finest hour". In his early years, he saw action in British India, the Anglo-Sudan War and the Second Boer War, where his exploits were recorded in his gripping dispatches. As First Lord of the Admiralty, he oversaw the disastrous Dardanelles campaign during the First World War before finding himself commanding a battalion on the Western Front – where his letters and reports captured the horror of the trenches. By war's end he was back in government – and once again showing off his oratory and wit on the Commons floor. And of course, beyond the Second World War, he didn't retire: as Leader of the Opposition, he continued to influence world affairs, becoming prime minister again in 1951.

Capturing the scope of Churchill's long and colourful career, this collection of his sharpest observations and funniest asides alongside his most stirring oratory and insights will amuse, inspire and uplift in equal measure.

CHAPTER
ONE

BRITISH
BULLDOG

66

We must just KBO.

99

A favourite maxim, delivered to friends and family – "Keep buggering on"

"

The maxim of the British people is, 'Business as usual'.

"

Speech at Guildhall, London, 1914

The nose of the bulldog has been slanted backwards so that he can breathe without letting go.

Speech at the London Opera House, 11 September 1914

66

Now is the time at last to rouse
the nation... We should lay aside
every hindrance and endeavour by
uniting the whole force and spirit
of our people to raise again a great
British nation standing up before
all the world; for such a nation,
rising in its ancient vigour, can even
at this hour save civilisation.

99

House of Commons, 24 March 1938

66

In the British Empire we not only look out across the seas towards each other, but backwards to our own history, to Magna Carta, to Habeas Corpus, to the Petition of Right, to Trial by Jury, to the English Common Law and to Parliamentary democracy. These are the milestones and monuments that mark the path along which the British race has marched to leadership and freedom.

99

Speech at the Canada Club, London, 20 April 1939

66
This is no time for ease and comfort. It is the time to dare and endure.

99

Speech at the Free Trade Hall, Manchester, 27 January 1940

Let us go forward together in all parts of the Empire, in all parts of the island. There is not a week, nor a day, nor an hour to lose.

Speech at the Free Trade Hall, Manchester, 27 January 1940

66

Today is Trinity Sunday. Centuries
ago, words were written to be
a call and a spur to the faithful
servants of Truth and Justice:
'Arm yourselves, and be ye men
of valour, and be in readiness for
the conflict; for it is better for us
to perish in battle than to look
upon the outrage of our nation and
our altar. As the will of God is in
Heaven, even so let it be.'

99

First broadcast as prime minister,
19 May 1940

We shall not flag or fail. We shall go on to the end. We shall fight in France, we shall fight on the seas and oceans, we shall fight with growing confidence and growing strength in the air. We shall defend our island, whatever the cost may be...

...We shall fight on the beaches, we shall fight on the landing-grounds, we shall fight in the fields and in the streets, we shall fight in the hills. We shall never surrender....

99

Following the evacuation of Allied troops from Dunkirk, House of Commons, 4 June 1940

Perhaps it will come tonight.
Perhaps it will come next week.
Perhaps it will never come.
We must show ourselves equally
capable of meeting a sudden violent
shock or, what is perhaps a harder
test, a prolonged vigil. But be the
ordeal sharp or long, or both, we
shall seek no terms, we shall tolerate
no parley; we may show mercy – we
shall ask for none...

Broadcast to the nation, 14 July 1940

66

…we would rather see London laid in ruins and ashes than that it should be tamely and abjectly enslaved.

99

House of Commons, 14 July 1940

Far be it from me to paint a
rosy picture of the future…
But I should be failing in my duty
if, on the other side, I were not
to convey the true impression,
that this great nation is getting
into its war stride.

House of Commons, 22 January 1941

"
Give us the tools and we will finish the job.

"

Broadcast to the United States, London, 9 February 1941

We know that other hearts in millions and scores of millions beat with ours; that other voices proclaim the cause for which we strive; other strong hands wield the hammers and shape the weapons we need; other clear and gleaming eyes are fixed in hard conviction upon the tyrannies that must and shall be destroyed.

Speech at a luncheon in honour of the United States ambassador, London, 18 March 1941

66

This is no time for boasts or glowing prophecies, but there is this – a year ago our position looked forlorn and well nigh desperate to all eyes but our own. Today we may say aloud before an awe-struck world, 'We are still masters of our fate. We still are captain of our souls.'

99

House of Commons, 9 September 1941

Never give in – never, never, never, never, in nothing great or small, large or petty, never give in except to convictions of honour and good sense. Never yield to force; never yield to the apparently overwhelming might of the enemy.

Speech at Harrow School for boys (Churchill's former school), London, 29 October 1941

66

Do not let us speak of darker days:
let us speak rather of sterner days.
These are not dark days; these
are great days – the greatest days
our country has ever lived; and we
must all thank God that we have
been allowed, each of us according
to our stations, to play a part in
making these days memorable in
the history of our race. **99**

*Speech at Harrow School for boys
(Churchill's former school), London,
29 October 1941*

When I warned [the French] that Britain would fight on alone, whatever they did, their generals told their prime minister and his divided cabinet: 'In three weeks, England will have her neck wrung like a chicken.'

Some chicken... Some neck!

Speech at the Canadian Parliament, Ottawa, 30 December 1941

Difficulties mastered are
opportunities won.

Broadcast, London, 21 March 1943

This is your victory! It is the victory of the cause of freedom in every land. In all our long history we have never seen a greater day than this.

Speech at the Ministry of Health, London, 8 May 1945

66

I have an invincible confidence in the genius of Britain.

99

Election broadcast, 30 June 1945

When we look back on all the perils through which we have passed and at the mighty foes we have laid low and all the dark and deadly designs we have frustrated, why should we fear for our future? We have come safely through the worst.

First major speech as Leader of the Opposition, House of Commons, 16 August 1945

66

[The] British people have always been superior to the British climate. They have shown themselves capable of rising above it, and certainly they have derived from it many of those strong enduring principles and ways of life which make their existence in our island home different from any other community in the world. **99**

Speech at Woodford, Essex,
10 July 1948

We have surmounted all the perils and endured all the agonies of the past. We shall provide against and thus prevail over the dangers and problems of the future, withhold no sacrifice, grudge no toil, seek no sordid gain, fear no foe. All will be well.

Speech at Château Laurier, Ottawa, 9 November 1954

"

I have never accepted what many people have kindly said, namely that I have inspired the nation. It was the nation and the race dwelling all around the globe that had the lion heart. I had the luck to be called upon to give the roar.

"

Speech at his eightieth birthday celebration, Westminster Hall, London, 30 November 1954

CHAPTER
TWO

WORLD
VIEWS

It is very rarely that stubborn and unshaken Infantry meets equally stubborn and unshaken Cavalry. Usually either the Infantry run away and are cut down in flight, or they keep their heads and destroy nearly all the horsemen by their musketry. In this case, the two mighty walls clashed together with a mighty collision.

At the Battle of Omdurman in central Sudan as war correspondent for the Morning Post, *29 September 1898*

66

You must remember that this was three days after the fight, and that the sun had beaten down mercilessly all the time. Some of the wounded were very thirsty. It would have been a grateful sight to see a large bucket of clear, cool water placed before each shaking feverish figure. That or a nameless man with a revolver… would have seemed merciful.

99

Aftermath of the Battle of Omdurman in central Sudan, as war correspondent for the Morning Post, *6 October 1898*

66

Keep cool, men. This will be
interesting for my paper.

99

*After the train he was on was attacked
by Boer rebels during the Second Boer War,
South Africa, November 1899*

"
Here life itself, life at its best and healthiest, awaits the caprice of the bullet... Existence is never so sweet as when it is at hazard. **"**

On the Second Boer War, South Africa, 4 February 1900

66

Corpses lay here and there.
Many of the wounds were of a
horrible nature. The splinters and
fragments of the shell had torn
and mutilated in the most horrible
manner. I passed about two
hundred while I was climbing up.
There was, moreover, a steady
leakage of unwounded men of
all corps. Some of these cursed
and swore...

...Others were utterly exhausted and fell on the hillside in a stupor. Others again seemed drunk, though they had no liquor. Scores were sleeping heavily. Fighting was still proceeding, and stray bullets struck all over the ground... 99

Reporting on the ill-fated Battle of Spion Kop during the Second Boer War, Morning Post, *South Africa, 17 February 1900*

Death stood before me, grim, sullen Death, without his light-hearted companion, Chance. So I held up my hand, and, like Mr Jorrock's foxes, cried, 'Capivy'. Then I was herded with the other prisoners in a miserable group...

Describing his capture during the Second Boer War, New York Times, 3 June 1900

"

We have had a banquet tonight at the Bavarian palace. A crowd of princes & princelets & the foreign officers of various countries. It began at 6 p.m. & was extremely dull...

"

Letter to his wife, Clementine,
from Germany, 15 September 1909

Do not grieve for me too much…
Death is only an incident, & not the
most important… On the whole,
especially since I met you my darling
one, I have been happy, & you have
taught me how noble a woman's
heart can be. If there is anywhere
else, I shall be on the lookout for
you. Meanwhile look forward, feel
free, rejoice in Life, cherish the
children, guard my memory. God
bless you. Goodbye.

*Written to his wife, Clementine, on
leaving for the Western Front, 17 July 1915*

" There is more blood than paint upon these hands. All those thousands of men killed. We thought it would be a little job, and so it might have been if it had been begun in the right way. **"**

Following his resignation from the wartime cabinet in the wake of the Dardanelles disaster, November 1915

It is a wild scene... Filth and rubbish everywhere, graves built into the defences & scattered about promiscuously, feet & clothing breaking through the soil, water and muck on all sides; & about this scene in the dazzling moonlight troops of enormous rats creep & glide, to the unceasing accompaniment of rifle & machine guns & the venomous whining & whirring of the bullets which pass overhead.

Letter to his wife, Clementine, from the Western Front, 23 November 1915

66
War is declared, gentlemen,
on the lice.
99

Addressing the Sixth Royal Scots Fusiliers,
France, 1916

This war proceeds along its terrible path by the slaughter of infantry... I say to myself every day, 'What is going on while we sit here, while we go away to dinner or home to bed?' Nearly 1,000 men – Englishmen, Britishers, men of our race – are knocked into bundles of bloody rags every twenty-four hours, and carried away to hasty graves or to field ambulances...

House of Commons, 23 May 1916

"
Bolshevism is a great evil...
arisen out of great social evils.
"

House of Commons, 29 May 1919

The Dardanelles might have saved millions of lives. Don't imagine I am running away from the Dardanelles. I glory in it.

Campaign speech, Leicester, November 1923

66

India is a geographical term. It is no more a united nation than the Equator.

Speech at the Royal Albert Hall, London, 18 March 1931

99

Canada is the linchpin of the English-speaking world. Canada, with those relations of friendly, affectionate intimacy with the United States on the one hand and with her unswerving fidelity to the British Commonwealth and the Motherland on the other, is the link which joins together these great branches of the human family, a link which, spanning the oceans, brings the continents into their true relation…

Speech honouring Canadian prime minister Mackenzie King, London, 4 September 1941

66
Study history, study history.
In history lies all the secrets
of statecraft.

99

Speaking to United States presidential
speechwriter James Humes

CHAPTER
THREE

OBSERVATIONS

At Blenheim I took two very important decisions: to be born and to marry. I am happily content with the decisions I took on both those occasions.

Attributed

66
I like things to happen, and if they don't happen I like to make them happen.

99

Attributed

66

Ladies of the Empire,
I stand for Liberty!

99

*Churchill's first public speech, aged 19,
defending the right of ladies of "easy virtue"
to mingle with men in the Empire Theatre bar,
London, 1894*

66

Mr. Winston Churchill presents
his compliments to Mr. Winston
Churchill, and begs to draw
his attention to a matter which
concerns them both…

99

*Letter to American author Mr Winston
Churchill, proposing a solution for how
confusion over their names might be
avoided, 7 June 1899*

Sweet cat – I kiss your vision as it rises before my mind. Your dear heart throbs often in my own. God bless you darling, keep you safe & sound.

Kiss the P.K. for me all over.

Letter to his wife, Clementine, from Germany, referring to their first child, Diana, as "puppy-kitten", 15 September 1909

66 I have derived continued benefit from criticism at all periods of my life and I do not remember any time when I was ever short of it. **99**

House of Commons, 27 November 1914

[The] truth is incontrovertible. Panic may resent it, ignorance may deride it, malice may distort it, but there it is.

House of Commons, 17 May 1916

66

Painting is a friend who makes no undue demands, excites to no exhausting pursuits, keeps faithful pace even with feeble steps, and holds her canvas as a screen between us and the envious eyes of Time or the surly advance of Decrepitude.

99

On his hobby, painting,
Strand Magazine, *December 1921*

Words, which are on proper
occasions the most powerful
engines, lose their weight and
power and value when they are
not backed by fact or winged
by truth…

House of Commons, 22 April 1926

66

Although I had talked with him so seldom and never for a moment on equal terms, I conceived an intense admiration and affection for him and, after his early death, for his memory.

99

On his father, Lord Randolph Churchill, Strand Magazine, *February 1931*

In the twinkling of an eye, I found myself without an office, without a seat, without a party, and without an appendix.

Recalling losing his seat and having his appendix removed, Strand Magazine, *1931*

66

The whole history of the world is summed up in the fact that when nations are strong, they are not always just, and when they wish to be just, they are often no longer strong.

99

House of Commons, 26 March 1936

Nothing is more certain or more obvious than that recrimination or controversy at this time would be not only useless but harmful and wrong. What is done is done. What has been done or left undone belongs to history, and to history, so far as I am concerned, it shall be left.

Following the abdication of King Edward VIII, House of Commons, 10 December 1936

66
Criticism in the body politic is like pain in the human body. It is not pleasant, but where would the body be without it?

House of Commons, 27 January 1940

99

66

What a slender thread
the greatest of things can
hang by.

*Musing on the Battle of Britain,
Chequers, 10 August 1940*

66

History with its flickering lamp
stumbles along the trail of the
past trying to reconstruct its
success to revive the echoes
and kindle with pale gleams the
passions of former days.

99

*Speech following the death of former
prime minister Neville Chamberlain,
House of Commons, 12 November 1940*

I do not at all resent criticism,
even when, for the sake of
emphasis, it for a time parts
company with reality.

House of Commons, 22 January 1941

66

I am a child of the House of Commons. I was brought up in my father's house to believe in democracy. 'Trust the people' – that was his message… I owe my advancement entirely to the House of Commons, whose servant I am.

99

Speech to a Joint Session of the United States Congress, Washington DC, 26 December 1941

It is not given to us to peer into the mysteries of the future. Still, I avow my hope and faith, sure and inviolate, that in the days to come the British and American peoples will, for their own safety and for the good of all, walk together in majesty, in justice and in peace.

Speech to a Joint Session of the United States Congress, Washington DC, 26 December 1941

"

Stalin also left upon me the impression of a deep, cool wisdom and a complete absence of illusions of any kind. I believe I made him feel that we were good and faithful comrades in this war – but that, after all, is a matter which deeds, not words, will prove.

"

On Soviet leader Josef Stalin,
House of Commons, 8 September 1942

I have seen the king, gay, buoyant, and confident, when the stones and rubble of Buckingham Palace lay newly scattered in heaps upon its lawns.

"

On King George VI, Usher Hall, Edinburgh, 12 October 1942

66

I am certainly not one of those
who need to be prodded. In fact,
if anything, I am a prod.

99

House of Commons, 11 November 1942

There is only one thing worse
than fighting with allies, and that
is fighting without them.

Chequers, 1 April 1945

66

For us, it remains only to say that in Franklin Roosevelt there died the greatest American friend we have ever known, and the greatest champion of freedom who has ever brought help and comfort from the new world to the old.

99

On the death of United States president Franklin D. Roosevelt, House of Commons, 17 April 1945

I am ready to meet my Maker. Whether my Maker is prepared for the great ordeal of meeting me is another matter.

30 November 1949

66

I always try, especially in a new House of Commons, to study the opinions of those to whom I am opposed, their expressions and moods, so far as I can.

99

House of Commons, 24 April 1950

I have never considered myself
at all a good hater – though
I recognise that from moment to
moment it has added stimulus
to pugnacity.

House of Commons, 6 November 1950

❝

Madam, the whole nation is grateful to you for what you have done for us and to Providence for having endowed you with the gifts and personality which are not only precious to the British Commonwealth and Empire and its island home, but will play their part in cheering and in mellowing the forward march of human society all the world over.

❞

Addressing Queen Elizabeth II at Guildhall, London, 1951

The spectacle of a number of middle-aged gentlemen who are my political opponents being in a state of uproar and fury is really quite exhilarating to me. **99**

House of Commons, 21 May 1952

66
The power of man has
grown in every sphere except
over himself.

99

Speech in Stockholm,
10 December 1953

Change is unceasing and it is likely that mankind has a lot more to learn before it comes to its journey's end... We might even find ourselves in a few years moving along a smooth causeway of peace and plenty instead of roaming around on the rim of Hell.

Speech at Guildhall, London,
9 November 1954

"

I am an optimist – it does not seem to be much use being anything else – and I cannot believe that the human race will not find its way through the problems that confront it, although they are separated by a measureless gulf from any they have known before... Thus we may by patience, courage, and in orderly progression reach the shelter of a calmer and kindlier age.

"

Speech at Guildhall, London,
9 November 1954

I am not a pillar of the church
but a buttress – I support it
from the outside.

On religion, c.1954

66

My ability to persuade my wife
to marry me [was] quite my most
brilliant achievement.

99

Attributed

In the course of my life, I have
often had to eat my words, and
I must confess that I have always
found it a wholesome diet.

Attributed

66

The journey has been
enjoyable and well worth
the taking – once.

99

*On his deathbed to his son-in-law,
Christopher Soames, January 1965*

CHAPTER
FOUR

WAR TALK

We must not regard war with a modern power as a kind of game… A European war cannot be anything but a cruel, heartrending struggle [that ends] in the ruin of the vanquished and the scarcely less fatal commercial dislocation and exhaustion of the conquerors.

House of Commons, 13 May 1901

66
Once you are so unfortunate as to be drawn into a war, no price is too great to pay for an early and victorious peace.
99

House of Commons, 13 May 1901

'We are all together.' I use these words because this is a war in which we are all together – all parties, all classes, all races, all states, principalities, dominions and powers throughout the British Empire, we are all together.

*Speech at the London Opera House
in the early weeks of the First World War,
11 September 1914*

"

War today is bare – bare of profit and stripped of all its glamour. The old pomp and circumstance are gone. War now is nothing but toil, blood, death, squalor and lying propaganda.

"

Radio interview, New York,
10 March 1932

I would rather see another ten or twenty years of one-sided armed peace than see a war between equally well-matched powers…

House of Commons, 23 November 1932

66

I am quite certain that there is not a man on these benches who would not regard it as the dearest purpose of his life to keep the horrors of war away from the world... I believe that if any man knew that by having [his right hand] cut off he would gain such an assurance, he would be proud to endure the mutilation.

99

House of Commons, 10 March 1936

If we study the history of Rome and Carthage, we can understand what happened and why. It is not difficult to form an intelligent view about the three Punic Wars; but if mortal catastrophe should overtake the British nation and the British Empire, historians a thousand years hence will still be baffled by the mystery of our affairs...

…They will never understand
how it was that a victorious nation,
with everything in hand, suffered
themselves to be brought low,
and to cast away all that they had
gained by measureless sacrifice
and absolute victory – gone
with the wind!

99

*Lamenting Britain's inadequate response
to the Nazi threat, House of Commons,
24 March 1938*

The utmost [Prime Minister Neville Chamberlain] has been able to gain for Czechoslovakia… has been that the German dictator, instead of snatching the victuals from the table, has been content to have them served to him course by course.

Following the Munich Agreement, House of Commons, 5 October 1938

66

And do not suppose that this is the end. This is only the beginning of the reckoning. This is only the first sip, the first foretaste of a bitter cup, which will be proffered to us year by year unless by a supreme recovery of moral health and martial vigour, we arise again and take our stand for freedom as in the olden time.

99

Following the Munich Agreement,
House of Commons, 5 October 1938

Outside, the storms of war may blow and the lands may be lashed with the fury of its gales, but in our own hearts this Sunday morning there is peace. Our hands may be active, but our consciences are at rest.

On the outbreak of war, House of Commons, 3 September 1939

66
I cannot forecast to you the action of Russia. It is a riddle wrapped in a mystery inside an enigma.
99

Broadcast, London, 1 October 1939

I know of nothing more remarkable in our long history than the willingness to encounter the unknown, and to face and endure whatever might be coming to us, which was shown in September by the whole mass of the people of this island in the discharge of what they felt sure was their duty.

Speech at the Free Trade Hall, Manchester, 27 January 1940

66

...I have formed an administration
of men and women of every party
and of almost every point of view.
We have differed and quarrelled in
the past, but now one bond unites
us all: to wage war until victory
is won, and never to surrender
ourselves to servitude and shame,
whatever the cost and the agony
may be.

99

First radio broadcast as prime minister,
10 May 1940

…I have nothing to offer but blood, toil, tears and sweat. We have before us an ordeal of the most grievous kind. We have before us many long months of toil and struggle.

First speech as prime minister,
House of Commons, 13 May 1940

66

You ask what is our policy. I will say, it is to wage war with all our might, with all the strength that God can give us, to wage war against a monstrous tyranny. You ask what is our aim? I can answer in one word: Victory. Victory at all costs. Victory in spite of all terror. Victory however long and hard the road may be. For without victory there is no survival.

99

First speech as prime minister,
House of Commons, 13 May 1940

The whole fury and might of the enemy must very soon be turned on us. Hitler knows that he will have to break us in this island or lose the war. If we can stand up to him, all Europe may be free and the life of the world may move forward into broad, sunlit uplands. But if we fail, then the whole world… will sink into the abyss of a new Dark Age…

...Let us therefore brace ourselves to our duties, and so bear ourselves that if the British Empire and its Commonwealth last for a thousand years, men will still say, 'This was their Finest Hour.'

*Speech as Britain braced itself
following the fall of France,
House of Commons, 18 June 1940*

There are vast numbers... who will render faithful service in this war but whose names will never be known, whose deeds will never be recorded. This is a war of the Unknown Warriors; but let all strive without failing in faith or in duty, and the dark curse of Hitler will be lifted from our age.

BBC Broadcast, 14 July 1940

66

Never in the field of human conflict was so much owed by so many to so few.

99

Paying tribute to the Royal Air Force
for their service during the Battle of Britain,
House of Commons, 20 August 1940

Never will I believe that the soul of France is dead. Never will I believe that her place amongst the greatest nations of the world has been lost for ever!… Remember we shall never stop, never weary, and never give in… We seek to beat the life and soul out of Hitler and Hitlerism. That alone, that all the time, that to the end…

…Goodnight then: sleep to gather strength for the morning. For the morning will come. Brightly will it shine on the brave and true, kindly upon all who suffer for the cause, glorious upon the tombs of heroes. Thus will shine the dawn. Vive la France!

99

Broadcast to France, 21 October 1940

But time is short! Every month that passes adds to the length and to the perils of the journey that will have to be made. United we stand. Divided we fall. Divided, the dark age returns. United, we can save and guide the world.

Broadcast to America, 16 June 1941

"

Keep your souls clean from all contact with the Nazis; make them feel even in their fleeting hour of brutish triumph that they are the moral outcasts of mankind. Help is coming; mighty forces are arming in your behalf. Have faith. Have hope. Deliverance is sure.

"

Broadcast to the world, 24 August 1941

Since the Mongol invasions of Europe in the sixteenth century, there has never been methodical, merciless butchery on such a scale, or approaching such a scale.

Broadcast to the world, 24 August 1941

"

This is a strange Christmas Eve.
Almost the whole world is locked
in deadly struggle... Let the
children have their night of fun...
Let us grown-ups share to the full
in their unstinted pleasures before
we turn again to the stern task and
the formidable years that lie before
us, resolved that... these same
children shall not be robbed of
their inheritance...

"

Broadcast to the world from the
White House, 24 December 1941

Here's to 1942, here's to a year of toil – a year of struggle and peril, and a long step forward towards victory. May we all come through safe and with honour.

New Year toast to staff and reporters,
train en route to Ottawa from Washington DC,
1 January 1942

66

The Germans have received back again that measure of fire and steel, which they have so often meted out to others. Now this is not the end. It is not even the beginning of the end. But it is, perhaps, the end of the beginning.

99

Speech following the victory at
El Alamein in North Africa, Mansion House,
London, 10 November 1942

Here let me say how proud we ought to be, young and old alike, to live in this tremendous, thrilling, formative epoch in the human story, and how fortunate it was for the world that when these great trials came upon it, there was a generation that terror could not conquer and brutal violence could not enslave.

Speech at Harvard University,
6 September 1943

66
Let 'em have it. Remember this. Never maltreat the enemy by halves.

99

On giving orders for bombers to attack Berlin, 23 September 1943

This war effort could not have been achieved if the women had not marched forward in millions and undertaken all kinds of tasks and work for which any other generation but our own… would have considered them unfitted…

Speech at the Royal Albert Hall, London, 29 September 1943

66

We shape our buildings,
and afterwards our buildings
shape us.

99

*Following the complete destruction
of the Commons chamber in a bomb raid,
House of Commons (meeting in the House of
Lords), 28 October 1943*

When you have to hold a hot coffee-pot, it is better not to break the handle off...

On the Battle of Italy, House of Commons, 22 February 1944

66

We may allow ourselves a brief period of rejoicing; but let us not forget for a moment the toil and efforts that lie ahead… We must now devote all our strength and resources to the completion of our task, both at home and abroad. Advance, Britannia! Long live the cause of freedom! God save the King!

99

Broadcast from 10 Downing Street announcing the surrender of Germany, 8 May 1945

The [atomic] bomb brought peace, but men alone can keep that peace, and hence forward they will keep it under penalties which threaten the survival, not only of civilisation but of humanity itself.

House of Commons, 16 August 1945

66

Meeting jaw to jaw is better than war.

99

Washington DC, 26 June 1954

CHAPTER
FIVE

WORDS
WITH BITE

“
Personally, I think Lloyd George a vulgar, chattering little cad… **”**

Speaking to Conservative politician J. Moore Bayley, 23 December 1901

66

There was brilliancy in decay;
the human body preyed on itself
and gained feverish energy in
the process of exhaustion. When
expenditure increased, waste
increased.

99

On Austen Chamberlain,
House of Commons, 16 May 1904

Some people will deny anything, but there are some denials that do not alter the facts.

31 March 1910

66

Personally, I am in full agreement with the noble lord on this point, and I am glad that we have found a common ground to stand on, though it be only the breadth of a comma.

99

House of Commons debate concerning the punctuation used in prayer books, 7 July 1910

I never complain of hard words across the floor of the House, but I claim to be allowed to match them with arguments equal to the attack which has been made.

House of Commons, 4 April 1911

66

He is one of those orators of whom it was well said: 'Before they get up, they do not know what they are going to say; when they are speaking, they do not know what they are saying; and when they have sat down, they do not know what they have said.'

99

On Lord Charles Beresford,
House of Commons, 1912

Lenin was sent into Russia by the Germans in the same way that you might send a phial containing a culture of typhoid or cholera to be poured into the water supply of a great city...

On Russian revolutionary Vladimir Lenin, House of Commons, 5 November 1919

66

A perverse destiny has seemed to brood over the Rt Hon. Gentleman's career. All his life has been one long struggle to overcome the natural amiability of his character.

99

*On Labour MP Philip Snowden,
25 May 1925*

66
The Hon. Gentleman is trying to
win distinction by rudeness.
99

On Labour MP Hugh Dalton,
10 May 1926

66
Unteachable from infancy to tomb – there is the first and main characteristic of mankind.
99

Letter to Lord Beaverbrook,
21 May 1928

You cannot cure cancer by
a majority. What is needed is a
remedy.

House of Commons, 19 June 1930

66

The government... are defeated by thirty votes and then the prime minister rises in his place utterly unabashed, the greatest living master of falling without hurting himself, and airily assures us that nothing has happened.

99

On Prime Minister Ramsay MacDonald,
House of Commons, 21 January 1931

I remember when I was a child, being taken to the [circus], which contained an exhibition of freaks and monstrosities, but the exhibit... which I most desired to see was... 'The Boneless Wonder'. My parents judged that the spectacle would be too... revolting for my youthful eye and I have waited fifty years to see The Boneless Wonder sitting on the Treasury Bench.

On Prime Minister Ramsay MacDonald, House of Commons, 28 January 1931

66

It is alarming and also nauseating to see Mr Gandhi, a seditious Middle Temple lawyer, now posing as a fakir of a type well-known in the East, striding half-naked up the steps of the Vice-regal palace, while he is still organising and conducting a defiant campaign of civil disobedience, to parley on equal terms with the representative of the king-emperor.

99

On Mohandas Gandhi, the father of Indian independence, London, 23 February 1931

Chamberlain is a Birmingham town councillor who looks at our national affairs through the wrong end of a municipal drainpipe.

On Prime Minister Neville Chamberlain, c.1938

[That] was not an insuperable task, since I admired many of Neville's great qualities. But I pray to God in his infinite mercy that I shall not have to deliver a similar oration on Baldwin. That indeed would be difficult to do.

After being praised for his tribute to former prime minister Neville Chamberlain, 22 November 1940

I certainly deprecate any
comparison between Herr Hitler
and Napoleon; I do not wish
to insult the dead...

On Adolf Hitler, 19 December 1940

66

That he is a great man I do not deny, but that after eighteen years of unbridled power he has led your country to the horrid verge of ruin can be denied by none. It is one man who... has arrayed the trustees and inheritors of ancient Rome upon the side of the ferocious pagan barbarians.

99

On Italian prime minister Benito Mussolini, broadcast to Italy, 23 December 1940

He is a lunatic in a country of lunatics, and it would be a pity to move him.

Speaking of Sir Richard Stafford Cripps, ambassador to Russia, December 1940

66

There is a winter, you know, in Russia. For a good many months the temperature is apt to fall very low. There is snow, there is frost, and all that. Hitler forgot about this Russian winter. He must have been very loosely educated.

99

Broadcast, London, 10 May 1942

I am afraid I have rather exhausted the possibilities of the English language.

On being asked to comment on Pierre Laval, Vichy France's prime minister who was executed after the war, House of Commons, 29 September 1942

66

I brought him up from a pup,
but I never got him properly trained
to the house!

99

*Speaking of General Charles de Gaulle
in a meeting with the United States Senate,
May 1943*

This is the kind of tedious
nonsense up with which I
will not put!

*Margin note by Churchill in response
to a civil servant's memo objecting to the
ending of sentences with a preposition,*
New York Times, *28 February 1944*

66
Toilet paper too thin,
newspapers too fat!

99

On being asked if he had any complaints
about the United States, press conference,
September 1944

Let him go to hell – as soon as there's a vacant passage.

On author P.G. Wodehouse, who made anti-British broadcasts on German radio, 6 December 1944

66

I should think it was hardly possible to state the opposite of the truth with more precision.

99

On Labour MP Aneurin Bevan,
House of Commons, 8 December 1944

I do not challenge the Hon. Gentleman when the truth leaks out of him by accident from time to time.

On Labour MP Emanuel Shinwell, House of Commons, 8 December 1944

66
He has much to be
modest about.

99

*Responding to a comment from
President Truman that Clement Attlee seemed
a "modest man", March 1946*

Yes! Like the grub that feeds on the royal jelly and thinks it's a queen bee.

On being told that Prime Minister Attlee was doing a good job, 1946

❝
The English never draw a
line without blurring it.

❞

House of Commons, 16 November 1948

If Cat cares to come home, all is forgiven.

Note placed in the window of Churchill's home, Chartwell, after a pet cat ran away (it later returned), attributed

66

I was giving the Rt Hon. Gentleman an honourable mention for having, it appears by accident, perhaps not from the best motives, happened to be right.

99

On Labour MP Aneurin Bevan,
6 December 1951

66

Dull, Duller, Dulles.

On United States secretary of state,
John Foster Dulles, 1953

66

I drink and smoke and I am
200 per cent fit.

99

In response to General Montgomery's
comment, "I neither drink nor smoke and I am
100 per cent fit." (Memoirs of Field Marshal
Montogomery, *1958).*

CHAPTER
SIX

WISDOM

"

The main qualification for political office is the ability to foretell what is going to happen tomorrow, next week, next month and next year... And to have the ability afterwards to explain why it didn't happen.

"

On being asked by a journalist what qualities a politician should possess, 1902

66

I object on principle
to doing by legislation what
properly belongs to human good
feeling and charity.

99

Attributed, 1902

Taxes are an evil – a necessary evil, but still an evil, and the fewer we have of them the better.

House of Commons, 12 February 1906

66
Men will forgive a man anything
but bad prose.

99

Election speech, Manchester, 1906

A man must answer 'Aye' or 'No' to the great questions which are put, and by that decision he must be bound.

House of Commons, 15 November 1915

66
Honours should go where death
and danger go...

House of Commons, 24 July 1916

99

The glory of light cannot exist
without its shadows.

Strand Magazine, *March 1931*

66
Live dangerously; take things
as they come; dread naught,
all will be well.

99

Daily Mail, *5 January 1932*

Anyone can rat, but it takes a
certain amount of ingenuity
to re-rat.

Attributed

66
Danger gathers upon our path.
We cannot afford – we have
no right – to look back. We must
look forward.
99

Following the abdication of
King Edward VIII, House of Commons,
10 December 1936

The arts are essential to any complete national life. The State owes it to itself to sustain and encourage them... Ill fares the race which fails to salute the arts with the reverence and delight which are their due.

The Royal Academy, 30 April 1938

"
Of course I am an egotist. Where
do you get if you aren't?
"

Cabinet Room, Downing Street, 1940s

"

The only guide to a man is his conscience; the only shield to his memory is the rectitude and sincerity of his actions. It is very imprudent to walk through life without this shield, because we are so often mocked by the failure of our hopes... but with this shield... we march always in the ranks of honour.

"

Speech following the death of former prime minister Neville Chamberlain, House of Commons, 12 November 1940

"
The inherent vice of capitalism
is the unequal sharing of
blessings. The inherent virtue of
socialism is the equal sharing
of miseries.

"

House of Commons, 22 October 1945

Stilton and port are like man and wife. They should never be separated. 'Whom God has joined together, let no man put asunder.' No – nor woman either.

Attributed, 1946

"
You must sleep some time between lunch and dinner, and no halfway measures. Take off your clothes and get into bed. That's what I always do. Don't think you will be doing less work because you sleep during the day. That's a foolish notion held by people who have no imagination. **"**

Attributed, 1946

66

The bug seems to have caught my truculence. This is its finest hour.

99

On an infection that was resisting penicillin, 27 June 1946

66

No one pretends that democracy
is perfect or all-wise. Indeed it
has been said that democracy is
the worst form of government
except for all those other forms
that have been tried from
time to time…

99

House of Commons, 11 November 1947

66

It is easier to break crockery than to mend it.

99

*Conservative Women's Council,
London, 21 April 1948*

66

One must never be discouraged
by defeats in one's youth, but
continue to learn throughout
one's whole life.

99

University of Oslo, 12 May 1948

A nation without a conscience is a nation without a soul.

A nation without a soul is a nation that cannot live.

Broadcast, London,
16 September 1951

66

A prisoner of war is a man who tries to kill you and fails, and then asks you not to kill him.

99

Observer, *1952*

66

In war you can only be killed once,
but in politics many times.
99

Attributed

the little book of
ASTROLOGY

Published by OH!
20 Mortimer Street
London W1T 3JW

Text © 2020 OH!
Design © 2020 OH!

Disclaimer:

ISBN 978-1-91161-068-7

Editorial consultant: Sasha Fenton
Editorial: Sasha Fenton, Victoria Godden
Project manager: Russell Porter
Design: Ben Ruocco
Production: Rachel Burgess

A CIP catalogue record for this book is available from the British Library

Printed in China

10 9 8 7 6 5 4

the little book of
ASTROLOGY

Anna McKenna

contents

introduction

The astrology in this book is called sun sign astrology, and it is very easy to understand because you don't need astrology charts or any specialized knowledge. Here, you can learn about yourself and look into the natures of your friends, family and lovers. You can even work out why some people rub you up the wrong way.

Those who love astrology are always keen to point out that there is a lot more to it than the sun sign. The moon, the planets, the rising sign and so much else besides all have interesting things to show us – and there is also the predictive side of this fascinating subject to take on board.

This book will interest many of you just as it is; for others, it might just kick-start a real interest in astrology, and it may inspire you to look further into this enduringly fascinating subject.

ARIES

21 march – 19 april

aries

21 march – 19 april

symbol: **THE RAM**

ruling planet: **MARS**

element: **FIRE**

quality: **CARDINAL**

gemstone: **BLOODSTONE**

motto: **'I AM'**

8

positive qualities: active, pioneering, courageous and positive

negative qualities: impatient, impulsive, selfish and bossy

Aries is the first sign of the zodiac, associated with spring, new life and active energy. Ariens' approach to life is enthusiastic, but they can also be self-centred.

aries
THE RAM

Aries is symbolized by the Ram, an animal known for persistently head-butting its way through obstacles and fearlessly charging towards anything in its way. It is this direct and sometimes confrontational nature, which characterizes the Aries sign. There is forcefulness and a disregard for consequences, which can be an Arian's support or downfall.

ruling planet
MARS

The planetary ruler of Aries is red
hot Mars. The Romans worshipped
Mars as the god of war, and in Greek
mythology the equivalent was Ares.
Martian energy is aggressive and
confrontational. It symbolizes raw,
masculine energy and can move with
a formidable force. Arians possess this
warlike quality of their ruling planet.

aries is a
FIRE SIGN

With fire as its element, the sign of Aries has the dynamism to initiate action and bring an enlivening spark to any venture. The fire element gives Arians creativity and unrivalled enthusiasm. Arians have a generous spirit and warmth about them. However, when their fiery energy is thwarted, their tempers can be explosive.

♈

aries is a
CARDINAL
SIGN

Cardinal signs are leaders and initiators, and Aries leads in an inspiring and creative way. There is a need in an Arian's to put thoughts into action; they are guided by a desire to move forwards with purpose and intention in an energetic and sometimes impulsive manner.

aries
21 march – 19 april

aries at its best

At best, Aries is kind, warm and generous. Arians make loyal friends who can be trusted to freely offer their help and support. Aries loves very deeply and is fiercely protective of their loved ones. They are great at any gathering, bringing an element of sparkle with their sense of fun and lively humour.

Being the first of the twelve sun signs, Aries is sometimes referred to as the infant of the zodiac, and they can display a childlike innocence in their approach to life. This quality makes them refreshingly honest and trusting. They are not afraid of the unknown and make wonderful travelling companions, as they happily embrace the spirit of adventure.

aries at its worst

Aries likes to get things done and finds it difficult to understand people who do not have the same drive. When they feel blocked in any way, they tend to charge ahead with great force, like the ram, attempting to eradicate obstacles. They can become bossy, selfish and angry towards anyone who does not share their vision.

Aries lacks patience and can quickly become hot-tempered. Usually their tempers cool quickly, however, as they focus on their next move. They can feel insecure when their needs are not met, or when they feel unloved or unappreciated. When this happens, they become self-centred and demand a lot of reassurance.

aries
IN LOVE

Fiery and passionate, the Arian falls in love quickly, often taking the other person by surprise at their speedy and direct approach. An Aries gives with an open heart and is a spontaneous and fun lover. However, they can become selfish as time progresses and lose interest in the relationship if the passion wanes.

♈

aries
AT WORK

An Aries is an asset to any team, as they are enthusiastic and contribute creative ideas. Their ability to follow up on ideas or check finer details is weak, however, as they tend to lose focus. They make good bosses, as they are natural leaders and motivators, comfortable with heading up a group of people.

how to
ATTRACT
and KEEP
an aries

In relationships, you need to match their level of enthusiasm and appreciate the joys of life. An Aries does not tolerate dishonesty, disloyalty or mean-spiritedness. Be aware that they are sensitive and hurt easily, despite all their bravado. Keep the passion alive and treat them with kindness.

famous aries
PERSONALITIES

Robert Downey Jr, Lady Gaga,
Reese Witherspoon, Emma Watson, Alec
Baldwin, Victoria Beckham, Quentin Tarantino,
Elton John, Guccio Gucci

"My mission in life is not merely to
survive, but to thrive; and to do so
with some passion, some compassion,
some humour, and some style."

Maya Angelou,
Aries – author, poet, singer and civil rights activist

TAURUS

20 april – 20 may

taurus

symbol: **THE BULL**

ruling planet: **VENUS**

element: **EARTH**

quality: **FIXED**

gemstone: **SAPPHIRE**

motto: **'I HAVE'**

positive qualities: reliable, practical, nature-loving and sensual

negative qualities: stubborn, greedy, possessive and stingy

Taurus is an earthy, fixed sign, giving them a practical, nature-loving quality. However, they have a stubborn streak, which may lead to conflict with others.

taurus
THE BULL

Taurus is symbolized by the Bull, a formidable beast known for its strength and stamina. The Bull can patiently endure much and does not surrender easily. These traits are reflected in the Taurus, who is hardworking and persistent when necessary. When challenged in some way, they can react angrily and surprise those around them with a sudden dramatic outburst.

♉

ruling planet
VENUS

Venus is the planet of love, and those
under her rule are drawn to the finer
things in life. They have an innate need
for harmony and to be surrounded
by beauty and luxury. The Taurean
creates a comfortable home and
indulges in good food, socialising and
sensual pleasures.

taurus

20 april – 20 may

taurus is an
EARTH SIGN

The earthy Taurus is grounded
and steadfast and works hard to
realise their ambitions. They have an
unwavering nature and are systematic
in their approach to life. Taureans have
a deep appreciation of nature and find
being in the countryside replenishing.
When angered, the Taurus displays
a temper with the force of an
earthquake and just as destructive.

♉

taurus is a
FIXED SIGN

As a fixed sign, Taurus has great powers of concentration and can focus on a task with steady precision. Their stubbornness and obstinacy can sometimes be counter-productive. At times, it is impossible for them to consider an alternative point of view and they will have a blinkered approach to problem-solving.

taurus

taurus at its best

A happy Taurus is patient, kind and sociable. They are great hosts and enjoy inviting people to their comfortable homes to sample their wonderful cooking. They are considerate friends and can be relied upon to provide help when necessary. Their steady nature gives them a sense of calm, which is a comfort during stressful times.

Taureans value money and their possessions and are careful with both. They work towards sustaining a prosperous home and look after their natural environment with care. As the toddler of the zodiac, when they feel well fed, comfortable and loved, the Taurean is affectionate, charming and a delight to be around.

taurus at its worst

If you try to rush a Taurus into any decision or persuade them into believing your point of view, you will witness them stubbornly digging their heels in and not moving an inch. Their idea may not be the best one, but when a Taurean is fixed on something, they will be blind to alternatives.

If not checked, the Taurean's love of money and comfort can make them greedy and possessive. They can become selfishly focused on building their own empire, with little regard to others' needs. They can also become sluggish if they overindulge in the good things in life and stubbornly ignore advice to look after their health.

taurus
IN LOVE

Sentimental and romantic, a Taurean will pour plenty of love and affection into their relationships. They do not rush into romance, as they need to know that they have a firm foundation on which to build a lasting love. Taureans have great stamina and they make sensual and generous lovers.

♉

taurus
AT WORK

A Taurus has a methodical approach to work and likes to do a job thoroughly. They are often happiest when working on their own, as they dislike being distracted or disturbed by less focused colleagues. As bosses, they can be patient and encouraging, as long as their opinions are respected at all times and not challenged.

taurus

how to

ATTRACT

and KEEP

a taurus

A Taurus will appreciate a kind-hearted and patient person who is willing to share in life's pleasures. They do not like to be bossed around or taken for granted. Show a Taurean that you value what they can provide and that you match their commitment to building a solid relationship.

famous taurus
PERSONALITIES

Queen Elizabeth II, George Clooney,
Penelope Cruz, David Beckham, Andy Murray,
Billy Joel, Dev Patel, Adele, Mark Zuckerberg

"If you really want something, you can
figure out how to make it happen."

Cher,
Taurus – singer, actress

GEMINI

21 may – 20 june

gemini

21 may – 20 june

symbol:	# THE TWINS
ruling planet:	# MERCURY
element:	# AIR
quality:	# MUTABLE
gemstone:	# AGATE
motto:	# 'I COMMUNICATE'

positive qualities: versatile, friendly, expressive and witty

negative qualities: unreliable, deceptive, unpredictable and contradictory

Gemini is a highly communicative sign and interested in many different topics. Geminis are freedom-loving and fun company but can be a little too flighty and whimsical at times.

gemini
THE TWINS

Gemini is said to have a dual personality, symbolised by the Twins. This means that they can have a distinctly good side and an opposite, darker side to their character. If this inner duality is complementary, then this individual can be talented and versatile. However, if there is a tension between these sides, the personality can be split and contradictory.

ruling planet
MERCURY

The Roman god Mercury and his
Greek equivalent Hermes were
messengers to the gods. With wings
on their feet, they would swiftly
go about their business. Mercurial
energy is fast-moving and governs
communication and the intellect,
giving Geminis agile minds, racing
with ideas, and the ability to gather
information at high speed.

gemini is an
AIR SIGN

Being an air sign, Geminis need space and freedom to be content in life. They can remain detached from people and places, enjoying taking a momentary dip into what piques their interest, and then taking off again like a butterfly.

♊

gemini is a
MUTABLE SIGN

Incredibly versatile, Geminis do not become fixed to any particular point of view. They are able to move through life considering any given situation from multiple perspectives. They enjoy change, adapt easily to new environments and communicate openly with people from different walks of life. They have a chameleon-like quality, which can make it difficult for others to understand their true character.

gemini
21 may – 20 june

gemini at its best

Geminis are exciting playmates, full of sparkle
and fun. They are engaging conversationalists
as they are interested in so many different
topics. They are always open to new ideas and
delight in learning and sharing knowledge.
They have a fondness for travel as this satisfies
their passion for exploration and discovery.

A Gemini is witty, carefree, and able to
entertain others with ease. When you have
their attention, Geminis are personable,
charming and funny. They are great party
guests as they are talented at bringing people
together. Geminis have a genuine interest in
people and life, which keeps their minds lively
and their approach refreshingly youthful.

gemini at its worst

The duality of the Twins can make Geminis difficult to fathom at times. There can be an inner tension, which creates unpredictable and unsettling behaviour. Their need for freedom and variety can result in them avoiding commitments or not following through with their promises. They can be unsympathetic towards people they disappoint.

They tend to change their minds and lose interest easily, which makes them unreliable and sometimes deceptive. The Gemini's delight in knowing about people and situations can make them incorrigible gossips, who may add a few of their own embellishments to rumours. The flip side to their sparkly personality is sometimes gloomy and self-absorbed.

gemini
IN LOVE

Geminis are young at heart and have a playful, flirtatious approach to romantic relationships. Their quick-witted, mercurial energy keeps interaction lively. They enjoy sharing ideas and experiences and thrive on good company. If the relationship does not maintain a sense of fun, though, a Gemini will move on to the next encounter with a carefree and sometimes careless attitude.

⛢

gemini
AT WORK

A Gemini is a great team player who will enjoy contributing ideas in the work environment. They think innovatively and can be effective problem-solvers. However, they find it difficult to prioritize and can get distracted and lose focus. The Gemini boss is communicative and friendly but may fall short on what has been promised.

how to
ATTRACT
and # KEEP
a gemini

Geminis like to be intellectually challenged
and free to express themselves. They
respond poorly to anyone who tries to
force them into thinking in a certain way
or into a commitment they do not want.
They will quickly disappear if they feel
pressured in any way. Be interesting
and interested and give your Gemini
plenty of freedom.

famous gemini
PERSONALITIES

Angelina Jolie, Johnny Depp, Prince,
Kanye West, Naomi Campbell, Morgan
Freeman, Che Guevara, Bob Dylan,
Venus Williams

"Imperfection is beauty, madness is
genius and it's better to be absolutely
ridiculous than absolutely boring."

Marilyn Monroe,
Gemini – actress, singer, model

CANCER

21 june – 22 july

cancer

21 june – 22 july

symbol: **THE CRAB**

ruling planet: **THE MOON**

element: **WATER**

quality: **CARDINAL**

gemstone: **EMERALD**

motto: **'I FEEL'**

positive qualities: kind, empathetic, generous and loyal

negative qualities: moody, oversensitive, clingy and jealous

Cancer is a kind-hearted and affectionate sign, always willing to help others. However, a Cancer's strong emotions and sensitivity can result in erratic and moody behaviour.

cancer
THE CRAB

The crab has a hard shell, which protects its soft centre. Likewise, a Cancer will appear to be tougher than they really are, as they hide behind a strong exterior. A crab's sideways walk and ability to cling onto objects is reflected in Cancer's indirect approach and tenacity.

ruling planet
THE MOON

The Moon waxes and wanes, and it influences the tides as they rise and fall. This constant changing is a Cancerian trait, as their moods swing one way and then the other, their emotions either high or low. The Moon represents feminine power, which gives a Cancer their sensitivity and intuition.

cancer is a
WATER SIGN

The watery energy of this sign gives a Cancer the ability to access knowledge through their feelings and intuition. They can tune into people and atmospheres with ease, sensing others' inner thoughts and motives. Their emotions can become too strong and spill over, causing them to behave irrationally.

cancer is a
CARDINAL SIGN

Cancerians are leaders and instinctively strive towards taking action. Their intuition helps them to sense people's strengths, so they can bring out the best in them and lead a team successfully. They trust in their 'hunches', which often pay off in terms of how to push ahead and make things happen.

cancer

cancer at its best

Cancerians are kind and considerate and often put others' happiness before their own. This makes them good friends on whom others can rely for support and comfort. They have an excellent memory and will remember and celebrate special occasions with generosity and joy. They tend to have a 'loony' sense of humour, which can be surprisingly quirky.

Cancerians pour their energy into caring for others. A happy family and home-life are very important for them to feel secure. They will devote time to providing nourishing meals and cultivating a comfortable atmosphere. If they do not have their own family, they will contribute towards a community or lend support to a worthy cause.

♋

cancer at its worst

Ruled by the Moon, Cancerian moods
are ever-changing, which makes them
unpredictable. Their moodiness and over-
sensitivity can cause Cancers to be 'crabby'
and difficult company. Although they give a lot
to others, if this is not reciprocated, Cancer
becomes resentful and sarcastic. They can
withdraw when they feel hurt and withhold
their true feelings.

Like the crab, Cancers can cling onto
situations and people with great tenacity.
They can find it difficult to let go and move on
from heartbreak or past circumstances that
have caused them pain. Others can sometimes
feel smothered by Cancerians whose
insecurity makes them overly anxious about
receiving affection.

cancer
IN LOVE

Cancerianss are in love with the idea of love and will be loyal and affectionate partners. They delight in giving and caring, and will defend their lovers if they are under attack. Food and comfort feature prominently in Cancerians' romantic relationships and they adore spending time at home, cuddling on the sofa, which some may find smothering.

cancer
AT WORK

The Cancer person works well in a team, conscious of considering others' points of view and contributing constructively. Be aware of their moods, however, as there may be times when they want to be left alone. As bosses, Cancerians may swing from being sympathetic to quite ruthless. They are shrewd in business and very good at handling finances.

how to
ATTRACT
and KEEP
a cancer

Cancers thrive on loving attention and kindness. They find humour in the most unexpected places and need to express their delight in the absurdities of life. They are easily hurt if they feel neglected or deceived in any way. Show sincere affection and lots of appreciation and you will be able to keep your Cancer sweet.

famous cancer
PERSONALITIES

Tom Cruise, Diana Princess of Wales,
Elon Musk, Lana Del Rey, Sylvester Stallone,
Tom Hanks, Linda Ronstadt, Priyanka Chopra,
Ricky Gervais

"If you want the cooperation of
humans around you, you must make
them feel important, and you do this
by being genuine and humble."

Nelson Mandela,
Cancer – President of South Africa, anti-apartheid activist,
philanthropist

LEO

23 july – 22 august

leo

23 july – 22 august

symbol:	**THE LION**
ruling planet:	**THE SUN**
element:	**FIRE**
quality:	**FIXED**
gemstone:	**ONYX**
motto:	**'I WILL'**

♌

positive qualities: warm, determined, ambitious and generous

negative qualities: proud, arrogant, stubborn and domineering

Leos are friendly and exciting characters, creative and positive in their outlook. However, their instinctive need to be the best means that they can be inconsiderate and overlook others.

leo
THE LION

Leos are royalty, symbolized by the Lion, so they will be king or queen of their domain. The have a proud air and expect to be respected and adored. When treated with love and made to feel important, they can be affectionate and kind. However, when challenged, they roar with anger.

♌

ruling planet
THE SUN

The Sun gives life and light to the universe and, likewise, Leos can bestow benevolence on those around them. Solar energy is fiery and constant, giving Leos creative stamina. Their sunny disposition spreads warmth and optimism but their fire can also become overwhelming and turn to arrogance.

leo

leo is a
FIRE SIGN

The fire element gives Leo its creative spark and the determination to rise to great heights of success. They are driven by the flames of ambition, and strive towards excellence. Fire needs freedom to express itself, and can be an explosive force if confined, or if others try to put it down.

♌

leo is a
FIXED SIGN

Leos can be strong-willed and determined, focusing on goals with dedication. They are not easily swayed, trusting in their abilities to overcome obstacles in their own way. They can be stubborn in their approach, not listening to advice or allowing others to put them off their dreams.

leo

leo at its best

A Leo is great to have on your side. They will gladly offer you help and advice and sincerely want the best for their family and friends. They enjoy being surrounded by positive people; are generous hosts and popular socialites. Their charm and optimism are engaging, and they make friends with ease.

Leos have a practical side to their nature and can be depended on to be problem-solvers. Their creative streak is inspiring, and Leos can excel in the arts and in the world of entertainment. They radiate warmth and kindness and will openly share their time and possessions. Dignity and confidence are also innate strengths.

♌ leo at its worst

A Leo can have a domineering and ruthless approach towards those who provoke or challenge them. Its pride can become overbearing and turn into arrogance and disdain for others' weaknesses. When they do not feel appreciated or respected, they make their displeasure known by behaving in a bad-tempered manner.

Leos can be extravagant and careless in the way that they spend money to satisfy their need for luxury. They can be vain and demanding, finding it difficult to understand those who do not acknowledge their superiority. Their stubborn streak can be counter-productive as they sometimes refuse to compromise or accept others' points of view.

leo
IN LOVE

Always the romantic, Leos delight in showering their romantic partners with gifts and celebrations. They believe in doing things in style and will not spare any expense in making sure that their romance is full of lavish experiences. They may be possessive at times and like to take charge, which can be problematic for some.

♌

leo
AT WORK

Leos work with steady focus and determination when a project interests them. They need to express creativity and like to be part of organizing teams of people. As bosses, Leos are responsible and organized, inspiring others to do their best and succeed. They have little time for those without ambition.

leo

how to
ATTRACT
and KEEP
a leo

Leos thrive on praise and love to know that they are adored by everyone. They need a partner they can feel proud of – someone who has dignity and style. Leos will not tolerate infidelity or a lack of morals. They will remain faithful and fulfilled if loved with warmth and respect.

♌

famous leo
PERSONALITIES

Jennifer Lopez, Barack Obama, Sandra Bullock,
Roger Federer, Ben Affleck, Robert De Niro,
Daniel Radcliffe, Alfred Hitchcock,
Helen Mirren

"I stand for freedom of expression,
doing what you believe in and going
after your dreams."

Madonna,
Leo – singer, songwriter, actress

VIRGO

23 august –
22 september

♍

virgo

symbol: **THE VIRGIN**

ruling planet: **MERCURY**

element: **EARTH**

quality: **MUTABLE**

gemstone: **CARNELIAN**

motto: **'I ANALYSE'**

♍

positive qualities: honest,
hardworking, meticulous and helpful

negative qualities: fussy,
distrustful, critical and
a hypochondriac

Virgos are kind-hearted and
instinctively want to serve others. They
patiently perform daily tasks well. They
can be overly critical of those who do
not share their goal for perfection.

virgo
THE VIRGIN

The Virgin rules over the harvest and is represented bearing the fruits of hard labour. She can deny herself gain and pleasure for the sake of providing for and serving others. Virgos, like the Virgin, have a pure and devoted approach to life; selflessly pouring energy into projects which they see will benefit the world at large.

♍

ruling planet
MERCURY

Mercury rules the mind and ways of thinking and learning. Virgos are known for their analytical skills and ability to focus on details. Mercurial energy can process information quickly, giving Virgos the ability to efficiently discern what is important in any given situation. They love reading and often have a large number of books.

virgo

23 august – 22 september

virgo is an
EARTH SIGN

The earthy Virgo is grounded in their daily routines and work. They strive to realize ambitions with a steady and methodical approach and ensure that foundations are solid before moving on with a project. They enjoy being in nature and working with their hands, fixing things or building something useful.

♍

virgo is a
MUTABLE SIGN

Virgos are extremely adaptable and can move from place to place with ease. They do not get too attached to people and can form new friendships in a variety of environments. They instinctively need time and space to be on their own, sometimes seeking a hermit's existence.

virgo

virgo at its best

With their need to serve and ability to devote themselves to daily tasks, Virgos can work tirelessly towards the common good. They have a modest air and do not seek praise, but rather remain in the background, quietly getting on with things. They make considerate friends and wonderful hosts, delighting in entertaining with perfection.

Their interests are varied, and they enjoy intelligent conversation with those who share their keen sense of observation. Virgos excel at anything that involves working with their hands, especially if they are producing something useful. They can be artistic and especially good at craftwork. Virgos are health-conscious and may have a healing quality about them.

♍

virgo at its worst

Virgos strive for perfection and can be overly
critical of those who fall short of their high
standards. Their cool and analytical approach
to life can be viewed as uncaring by some and
they can lack sympathy at times. Their interest
in health can become obsessive, which causes
them to become self-centred hypochondriacs.

Virgos are instinctively sceptical and not
readily convinced. They require considerable
evidence in order to believe in something
whole-heartedly. They are fussy and can be
difficult to please. At times, their tendency
for caution makes them slow to act or accept
new ideas. They find it difficult to understand
those who do not share their tendency for
abstinence.

virgo
IN LOVE

Virgos are faithful and devoted lovers. It may take them some time to fall in love, but once they do, they give of themselves sincerely. They will enjoy sharing the daily routine and delight in simple, earthy pleasures. Virgos expect their partners to behave with decorum and do not have time for anyone overly emotional.

♍

virgo
AT WORK

A Virgo colleague is fastidious and systematic in their approach. They like to share ideas in a clear and focused way and do not tolerate distractions. They have a talent for prioritizing and efficiency. A Virgo boss will expect work to high standards and may be openly critical of those who lack their sense of dedication.

virgo

23 august – 22 september

how to
ATTRACT
and KEEP
a virgo

The Virgo person is attracted to people who present themselves well and who can talk intelligently. They also like to indulge their interests in visiting different places and like a partner to share this spirit of discovery. Virgos will appreciate being given the space to be themselves, and time to spend on their own.

♍

famous virgo
PERSONALITIES

Cameron Diaz, Keanu Reeves, Stephen King,
Mother Theresa, Tim Burton, Van Morrison,
Freddie Mercury, Tom Hardy, Salma Hayek

"I never said, 'I want to be alone,'
I only said, 'I want to be left alone.'
There is all the difference."

Greta Garbo,
Virgo - actress

LIBRA

23 september –
22 october

libra

symbol: **THE SCALES**

ruling planet: **VENUS**

element: **AIR**

quality: **CARDINAL**

gemstone: **CHRYSOLITE**

motto: **'I BALANCE'**

positive qualities: charming, fair,
friendly and co-operative

negative qualities: indecisive, lazy,
argumentative and unfeeling

Librans are pleasant and sociable.
They have a good sense of justice and
strive for what is right. They delight
in intellectual discussion but can be
argumentative at times.

libra
THE SCALES

The Scales represent justice and balance, which gives Librans an instinctive need for harmony and fairness. They are advocates of what is morally right and find it difficult to function in an environment in which there is imbalance. Librans are painstaking about weighing up different sides of a situation, before reaching a well-measured conclusion.

♎

ruling planet
VENUS

Venus is the planet of love and beauty; two aspects of life, which Librans need in order to feel content. They enjoy creating a beautiful home and surrounding themselves with objects of art. Librans rule relationships and need to have a significant partner in their lives. They are also highly sociable and delight in merrymaking.

libra
23 september – 22 october

libra is an
AIR SIGN

In spite of being sociable, Librans have an ability to remain detached from people, maintaining a sense of independence. In this way they do not get too involved in others' lives as they prefer to be free of obligations and commitments. They need plenty of mental stimulation and thrive on debates and discussions.

♎︎

libra is a
CARDINAL SIGN

The cardinal quality of this sign makes Librans good leaders who inspire people to follow them using clear logic and a measured approach to situations. Their ability to assess different factors in a balanced and accurate way gives Librans an advantage in creating solutions and strategies.

libra at its best

Librans strive for peace and harmony and can be good arbitrators. They are fair and they like equality, sometimes being spokespeople for worthy causes and representing the disadvantaged. Librans are good listeners and they enjoy offering advice and discussing options. In this way, they make helpful friends who can be relied upon for thoughtful guidance.

They have a love of beauty and the arts and are talented at creating beautiful environments where everything is balanced and harmonious. Librans pay attention to their appearance and are instinctively stylish. They are fond of social gatherings and are charming company, able to keep the conversation interesting and alive.

libra at its worst

Librans can be unreliable and unpredictable. Their need for freedom can make it difficult for them to make commitments. They can be lazy, preferring to relax and socialise rather than spending time doing tedious chores. Librans may be manipulative as they are skilled at knowing how to make people react.

Their need to consider all sides of a story before making a decision may be counter-productive at times and frustrating for others. Librans' detached approach could be perceived as unsympathetic as they move away from difficult situations and people with ease. They can be disloyal and contradictory, on your side one minute and then opposing you the next.

libra

libra
IN LOVE

Librans instinctively need to be in a romantic relationship and they make charming and considerate partners. They strive for harmony and enjoy sharing the finer things in life with a loved one. They can be rather fickle, however, and switch from one romance to another with little hesitation.

♎︎

libra
AT WORK

Librans make co-operative colleagues
who enjoy creative problem-solving
and forming alliances. They will
be friendly and helpful and excel
at working in a different range of
locations. As bosses, they will be
fair and lead with a calm approach,
although they may take a long time to
make decisions.

libra

how to
ATTRACT
and KEEP
a libra

Librans like to have a partner who is their equal in behaviour and appearance. They delight in lively conversation and need to be with someone who provides intellectual stimulation. They fall for people who make themselves and their environment attractive. Librans can leave a relationship suddenly if it starts to become too predictable.

♎

famous libra

PERSONALITIES

Kate Winslet, Bruce Springsteen,
John Lennon, Catherine Zeta-Jones,
Oscar Wilde, Margaret Thatcher, Will Smith,
Ralph Lauren, Gwyneth Paltrow

"Happiness is when what you think,
what you say, and what you do are
in harmony."

Gandhi,
Libra – lawyer, anti-colonial nationalist, political ethicist

SCORPIO

23 october –
21 november

scorpio

symbol:	# THE SCORPION
ruling planet:	# PLUTO
element:	# WATER
quality:	# FIXED
gemstone:	# BERYL
motto:	# 'I DESIRE'

♏

positive qualities: determined, loyal, passionate and imaginative

negative qualities: jealous, possessive, vengeful and obsessive

Scorpios are passionate and intense. They have a strong will and work determinedly towards their goals. They can be caring friends, but harsh enemies who do not forgive and forget.

scorpio
THE SCORPION

Like the scorpion, Scorpios are hardy and resourceful, able to function in difficult environments and circumstances. There is little to distract them from their path once they have decided to do something. Scorpios react strongly to wrongdoing and can sting with their words and actions.

♏

ruling planet
PLUTO

God of the underworld, Pluto guards
the secrets of the murky depths of
life. This gives Scorpios a fascination
for subjects that are dark, taboo and
mysterious. They delve into life with
intensity and they are truth-seekers.
Scorpios are fearless when it comes
to facing the less appealing aspects of
human nature and existence.

scorpio is a
WATER SIGN

The water quality of this sign makes Scorpios imaginative and sensitive. Theirs is still water that has hidden depths and is able to keep many secrets. There is a magnetic, mysterious side to Scorpios, which can be both alluring and repelling, causing others to react strongly to their presence.

♏

scorpio is a
FIXED SIGN

A Scorpio needs steady routine and does not like sudden changes. They are steadfast and able to carry on under difficult conditions, overcoming obstacles with a strong will. They can show great determination when they have a dream to fulfil, and they will not be distracted by those less committed.

scorpio at its best

When you are in need, call on a Scorpio friend. Once people have earned their friendship, they will do almost anything for their pals. Their loyalty is guaranteed because when a Scorpio commits to something or someone, they do so absolutely. This is the sign of no half-measures; it really is all or nothing.

Passionate and imaginative, Scorpios are interesting company and delight in meaningful discussions. They are genuinely fascinated by people's lives and thrive on finding out what motivates those around them. They can have psychic abilities and enjoy subjects like the occult and psychology. Scorpios are sincere and caring, and are able to handle difficult situations with sensitivity.

♏

scorpio at its worst

Scorpios hate with an intensity and are unwavering in seeking revenge if they believe they have been mistreated. They will use harsh words and actions, making them ruthless enemies. Their strong will may be counter-productive if they stubbornly persist in pursuing something unnecessarily. Their instinctive need to discover things about people may lead to obtrusive behaviour.

Obsessing about matters is a Scorpio weakness that can lead to their own misery. They may have a self-destructive streak and are not afraid to express their darker nature. This can sometimes make them slightly morbid in their outlook. They have a powerful presence, so when they are in a bad mood; everyone around them is made aware of it.

scorpio
IN LOVE

Scorpios love with passion and devotion. They will totally commit themselves to another, sharing the good and the bad aspects of life. They are driven by an instinctive desire for deep and meaningful relationships, wasting little time on anyone who is less committed. Scorpios will end a relationship with a dramatic intensity if they feel deceived.

♏

scorpio
AT WORK

Scorpios work steadily and have great powers of concentration and focus. They make committed colleagues who will sometimes do more than expected, pouring energy and drive into projects. They will be supportive and enjoy sharing creative ideas. The Scorpio boss will be considerate but will expect you to work hard and with absolute dedication.

how to
ATTRACT
and KEEP
a scorpio

To attract a Scorpio, be true to yourself, because they can spot a phoney person a mile away. They respond well to depth of character and sincerity in words and action. A Scorpio is content in a secure routine and enjoys sharing their life with someone who can match their passion and drive.

♏

famous scorpio
PERSONALITIES

Julia Roberts, Whoopi Goldberg,
Hillary Clinton, Bill Gates, Pablo Picasso,
Leonardo DiCaprio, Anne Hathaway,
Katy Perry, Matthew McConaughey

"The problem is not to find the
answer; it's to face the answer."

Terence McKenna,
Scorpio – author, lecturer, ethno-botanist, mystic

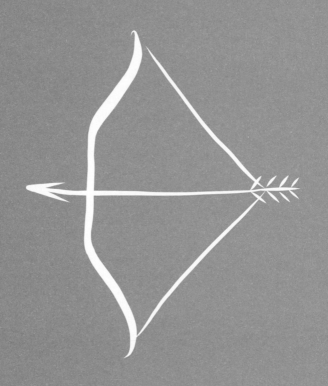

SAGITTARIUS

22 november –
21 december

sagittarius

22 november – 21 december

symbol: THE ARCHER

ruling planet: JUPITER

element: FIRE

quality: MUTABLE

gemstone: CITRINE

motto: ‘I PHILOSOPHIZE’

positive qualities: adventurous, fun-loving, optimistic and open-minded

negative qualities: restless, procrastinating, tactless and unreliable

Sagittarius is an exciting and expansive sign, charging ahead with enthusiasm and humour. They thirst for adventure, making them interesting company, but they can fall short of their promises.

sagittarius

22 november – 21 december

sagittarius
THE ARCHER

The Archer is energetic and dynamic.
He is half man, half horse, giving
Sagittarius a powerful, masculine
energy that thrives on movement and
challenge. There is an instinctive need
for freedom with this sign, as the
Archer does not like to be confined or
restricted in any way.

122

ruling planet
JUPITER

Jupiter is the planet of good fortune
and benevolence. In mythology, Jupiter
was referred to as Jove, the king of
the Roman gods. He was generally a
jovial and generous ruler but could
be ruthless when angered. Likewise,
Sagittarians are friendly and easy-
going, but do have a formidable
temper.

sagittarius

sagittarius is a
FIRE SIGN

Sagittarians are driven to be creative and adventurous. Their fiery nature gives them plenty of fearless energy to explore the world and spark motivation into those around them. Their flames may burn themselves out, however, and Sagittarius can lose enthusiasm and abandon projects and people.

sagittarius is a
MUTABLE
SIGN

The mutable quality makes Sagittarians friendly, helpful and communicative. They enjoy discussions and need the flexibility and space to move from one topic to the next and the freedom to express their sometimes unconventional views. While they like to associate with a variety of people, they may not form significant attachments.

sagittarius

sagittarius at its best

A Sagittarian is an exciting friend with whom to share adventures. They have a considerable capacity for pleasure and they can sometimes overdo things. They make great travel companions and they feel at home in different places. Sagittarians have a talent for immersing themselves in foreign cultures with ease and then happily entertain people with stories of their escapades.

Sagittarius is a lucky sign because Jupiter is the planet of good fortune. This gives them a delightfully carefree energy, which is both kind-hearted and open-minded. They are the life-long learners and make gifted teachers, with a hunger for knowledge. Sagittarians can be charming and funny and always light up a room with their fiery sparkle.

sagittarius at its worst

A Sagittarius person loves a debate, but they can sometimes become argumentative and persist in expressing their opinions long after others have lost interest. There is an antagonistic side to their nature and they can provoke a disagreement unnecessarily. At times, they can be arrogant and dismissive, upsetting others with their tactless approach.

When they lack focus, the Sagittarius person can become restless and muddled, not knowing what to do with all their energy. This leads to procrastination and a tendency not to follow through with commitments. They believe that there is always something better somewhere else, which means that they can wander the world aimlessly.

sagittarius
IN LOVE

The Sagittarian lover is generous and fun-loving, pouring fiery energy into their relationships. When you are their number one, you will be showered with attention and adored. They do not tolerate judgemental people or anyone who wants to rein them in. A Sagittarian needs freedom and may become restless in a relationship, leaving quite abruptly.

sagittarius
AT WORK

Sagittarians thrive in a stimulating work
environment, which gives them the
opportunity to meet different people,
use their sharp mind and ideally travel.
They find monotony and being in one
place stifling, which can affect their
performance. A Sagittarius boss will be
encouraging and generous but may
lose their temper with those who are
slower than they are, or less active
and adaptable.

how to
ATTRACT
and KEEP
a sagittarius

The Sagittarius person will be attracted by someone who is fun, energetic and independent. They really want a playmate, someone with whom they can share adventures, and who appreciates their carefree approach. They do not respond well to moodiness or being tied down. Be free-spirited and open to secure their affections.

famous sagittarius
PERSONALITIES

Brad Pitt, Katie Holmes, Bruce Lee,
Taylor Swift, Ozzy Osbourne, Frank Sinatra,
Winston Churchill, Woody Allen,
Scarlett Johansson.

"Travel is fatal to prejudice, bigotry,
and narrow-mindedness, and many
of our people need it sorely on
these accounts."

Mark Twain,
Sagittarius – author, publisher, lecturer

CAPRICORN

22 december –
19 january

♑

capricorn

symbol: ## THE SEA GOAT

ruling planet: ## SATURN

element: ## EARTH

quality: ## CARDINAL

gemstone: ## RUBY

motto: ## 'I MASTER'

♑

positive qualities: resourceful, hardworking, responsible and practical

negative qualities: bossy, pessimistic, cynical and egotistical

Capricorn is a determined sign, being single-minded in their ambitions. Their motivation and strategic approach are admirable, although they can be domineering at times.

capricorn
THE SEA GOAT

The mythical sea goat has the head and body of a mountain goat and the tail of a fish. Like the mountain goat, Capricorns move towards their goals with a determined and sure-footed approach, overcoming obstacles and adhering to their path. They can also adapt if necessary, diving into deep waters like the fish.

♑

ruling planet
SATURN

Saturn is the planet of hard lessons, limitations and time. This planet's energy is disciplinarian, forcing Capricorns to work diligently for everything they earn during their lifetime. Saturn also gives Capricorns maturity and wisdom from an early age and an ability to plan for the long-term.

capricorn
22 december – 19 january

capricorn is an
EARTH SIGN

The earthy quality of this sign gives Capricorns a grounded steadiness. They approach life methodically and they are very practical. Capricorns enjoy sensual, earthly pleasures and the finer things in life. The earth element gives an instinctive desire to accumulate possessions and acquire financial security.

♑

capricorn is a
CARDINAL
SIGN

Capricorns lead by example, inspiring others to follow their hardworking and dedicated approach. As a cardinal sign, they are driven to take action and make things happen. Capricorns are effective strategists and they aim high. They may be unforgiving leaders at times and can be selfish in their drive to get ahead.

capricorn

capricorn at its best

Capricorns have a wry sense of humour
and can be merry, like the god Pan who is
associated with the sign. Their dry wit makes
them enjoyable company and they will thrive
on intelligent conversation. They have a good
sense of style and are well-groomed, opting to
invest in fine-quality outfits.

Capricorns take responsibility for
themselves and they are fiercely independent.
They have a kind streak, which means that
they take care of others and are especially
loyal and giving to their families. They can be
relied on to offer substantial assistance when
others are in need, and generously to share
their wealth and possessions.

ꑉ

capricorn at its worst

At times, Capricorns can be domineering
and egotistical, putting their ambitions first.
They will determinedly pursue their goals,
overlooking other people. Their thirst for
success can become their main driving force,
making it difficult for them to pay attention to
other areas of life. They can lack patience with
people who do not share their outlook.

Capricorns can be vain and image-
conscious. They can be expedient and
manipulate their way into circles that they think
may benefit them in some way. Capricorns
sometimes lack imagination, and are so
grounded in reality that they can become dull.
They can live a monotonous life with only work
and success as the priorities. The worst thing
about them is that they are untrustworthy.

capricorn
IN LOVE

When a Capricorn falls in love, they will do so with great ardour. They will be devoted and faithful lovers and enjoy giving their partners the best of everything. They are not interested in short romances, but rather like to be in committed, long-term relationships. They can be quite jealous and possessive, though, guarding their lovers closely. They are often attracted to older partners.

♑

capricorn
AT WORK

Capricorns will be reliable and conscientious colleagues, usually taking on more responsibility than is necessary. They like to be in charge of projects, so work best as team leaders. They need the freedom to make decisions and devise strategies. Capricorn bosses are clear-thinking and fair but they make hard taskmasters.

how to
ATTRACT
and KEEP
a capricorn

Behave with decorum and keep yourself looking respectable if you want to attract a Capricorn. They need to be with a companion who inspires pride, and who complements them. Capricorns do not tolerate laziness or shoddy morals. Keep up with their high standards, and they will be devoted to you.

♑

famous capricorn
PERSONALITIES

Michelle Obama, Mel Gibson, Jim Carey,
Denzel Washington, the Duchess of
Cambridge, Mary J Blige, Ricky Martin,
Diane Keaton, Muhammad Ali

"However difficult life may seem,
there is always something you can
do or succeed at."

Stephen Hawking,
Capricorn – theoretical physicist, cosmologist, author

AQUARIUS

20 january – 18 february

aquarius

symbol: **THE WATER BEARER**

ruling planet: **URANUS**

element: **AIR**

quality: **FIXED**

gemstone: **GARNET**

motto: **'I KNOW'**

positive qualities: humanitarian, friendly, inventive and eclectic

negative qualities: obstinate, rebellious, aloof and opinionated

Aquarians have admirable intentions and adhere to their principles. They have strong ideas about how the world should be, but can be idealistic and stubborn in their views.

aquarius

THE WATER BEARER

The Water Bearer is depicted carrying a large jug of water, which he is pouring out onto the ground. This symbolizes a releasing of knowledge from a great container, through the air and onto the earth. Aquarians thirst for knowledge and are driven to share what they know with others, for the common good.

ruling planet
URANUS

Uranus is the planet of chaos and rebellion as it revolves in a different direction to other planets. This planet can cause sudden, unexpected events, and forcefully challenge us to depart from familiarity. Likewise, Aquarians like to see things in a different way, thriving on invention and an eccentric approach.

aquarius

aquarius is an
AIR SIGN

As an air sign, Aquarius is concerned with communication and the intellect. They have an instinctive need to express their opinions, which may sometimes be unconventional. Aquarians live in the world of ideas and theories. They will be interested in a great variety of topics and people.

aquarius is a
FIXED SIGN

The fixed quality of this sign makes Aquarians adhere to their viewpoints with determination. They have strong convictions, which they share passionately. It may take Aquarians some time to make a commitment, but once they do, they stay committed. They are not easily swayed or influenced by others and they have a stubborn streak.

aquarius

aquarius at its best

Aquarians are sociable and like to have a large,
eclectic circle of friends. They are supportive
and loyal and often like to defend those they
believe are vulnerable in some way. As they
have varied interests, they make interesting
and stimulating company. Their approach
to life is optimistic and they bring hope to
people when times are hard.

This sign has an instinctive desire to spread
goodness in the world and to bring people
together. They enjoy being active within a
community, contributing their energy into
group projects. They have lively minds and
thrive on intellectual pursuits. Aquarians are
inventive and creative and have a talent for
seeing things others miss.

aquarius at its worst

There is an obstinate streak in Aquarians, which can be counter-productive. They can become very fixed on a certain point of view, and can hang on to opinions that are no longer relevant. They can also be too rebellious, sometimes flouting authority without much thought. Their eccentric nature can make them difficult to understand.

Aquarians find it challenging to access and express their emotions, and can come across as aloof and uncaring. They are driven more by their minds than their hearts. They can be detached and act in an absent-minded way, lost in thought. They can be domineering and argumentative when others do not agree with their point of view.

aquarius
IN LOVE

Independent Aquarians need plenty of space within a relationship and are often more interested in a good friendship than a romantic commitment. Although capable of affection and loyalty, they may find it difficult to stay with one partner for very long. They can move on to the next project, person or worthy cause with ease.

aquarius
AT WORK

As a colleague, Aquarius is inventive and works well with technology. Their passion for sharing ideas is beneficial in a work environment and they will contribute thoughtfully. The Aquarian boss is fair and painstaking about looking after their employees' interests. However, they can be elusive and difficult to pin down.

how to
ATTRACT
and KEEP
an aquarius

Aquarians are attracted by intelligent and considerate people who share their humanitarian outlook. They need to be accepted for themselves and to be given absolute freedom. Aquarians respond poorly to anyone who is old-fashioned, or who maintains outdated opinions. They will stay with those who are interested in people, the world and the future.

158

famous aquarius
PERSONALITIES

Oprah Winfrey, Jennifer Aniston,
Michael Jordan, Ed Sheeran, Christian Bale,
Alicia Keys, Justin Timberlake, Harry Styles,
Ashton Kutcher

"I only have one ambition, y'know. I
only have one thing I'd really like to
see happen. I'd like to see mankind
live together – black, white, Chinese,
everyone – that's all."

Bob Marley,
Aquarius – singer, songwriter, musician

PISCES

19 february – 20 march

pisces

19 february – 20 march

symbol:	# THE FISH
ruling planet:	# NEPTUNE
element:	# WATER
quality:	# MUTABLE
gemstone:	# AMETHYST
motto:	# 'I BELIEVE'

positive qualities: compassionate,
imaginative, adaptable and creative

negative qualities: indecisive,
easily led, delusional and
temperamental

Pisceans are kind and sensitive, putting
others first. They are easy-going and
permissive, but this can sometimes
be to their detriment. They are
extremely intuitive.

pisces
THE FISH

The symbol of two fish, tied together and swimming in different directions, represents the fluidity of Pisces. They can adapt, but sometimes find it difficult to decide how to change in order to fit into a new environment. Pisceans can be slippery, which means they can easily wriggle out of unpleasant situations.

ruling planet
NEPTUNE

The Roman god Neptune ruled
over the deep, mysterious seas.
The Neptune energy is boundless
and powerful like the ocean, giving
Pisceans strong emotions that ebb,
flow and sometimes overwhelm
them. Neptune also represents the
unconscious, hidden realms that hold
great fascination for Pisceans.

pisces is a
WATER SIGN

The water element gives this sign sensitivity and gentleness. Pisceans are daydreamers who get lost in music, poetry and fantasy. Their powerful imagination rules over them to such an extent that sometimes they become detached from reality. They are highly intuitive and have psychic abilities, being able to tune into those around them.

H

pisces is a

MUTABLE
SIGN

This sign is mutable, which makes Pisceans friendly and expressive. They switch from one idea or dream to the next, without committing themselves. Pisceans have a chameleon-like quality that gives them a talent for blending in with people to the point where their identity is blurred.

pisces at its best

The Piscean's gentle and compassionate nature makes them caring and sympathetic friends. They enjoy discussions in which they can express their imaginative thoughts and nurture the ideas of others. They are creative, artistic and have a keen sense of what works, and they will readily help those in need and feel other people's pain.

Pisces is an intuitive sign, giving them the ability to respond sensitively to situations and help in an appropriate way. They are interested in mysticism and spirituality and have a genuine desire to inspire faith in humanity. Their friendships may be select, but they will be deep and sincere. Their best attribute by far is that they don't judge or put others down, they are never arrogant, and they make allowances for weakness in others.

pisces at its worst

The Piscean can become so overwhelmed by the weight of the world that they disappear into themselves. They will swim away and hide, sometimes becoming self-pitying and melancholic. When their strong emotions take over, Pisceans may become self-destructive and delusional, losing touch with reality. This makes it difficult for them to function.

Pisces has an elusive quality which people may find difficult to understand. They find it difficult to express what they feel and they can isolate themselves. They can be lazy, non-committal and deceptive. Pisceans lack a strong sense of identity and they can be moody and changeable, making it a challenge to relate to them at times.

pisces
IN LOVE

Pisces lovers are deeply romantic and enjoy creating and living out fantasies in their relationships. They have an instinctive need to freely share their emotions and thrive on getting to know their lover on a deep level. However, if they feel pressured in any way, they can take on the slippery quality of the fish and avoid commitments.

pisces
AT WORK

The Pisces colleague may be a daydreamer at work. They are friendly and helpful, often nurturing those who are less confident. They have plenty of ideas, and are amazingly creative, but they may be unrealistic. As a boss, they will be caring and particularly inspiring in careers connected to the arts. They may find decision-making a challenge.

how to
ATTRACT
and KEEP
a pisces

Appeal to a Piscean's imagination if you want to catch their eye. If you can inspire a fantasy in dress, behaviour or through what you say, Pisces will be interested. They dislike ordinary people or a routine life, and they need open communication. Be kind and romantic and they will respond well.

famous pisces
PERSONALITIES

Daniel Craig, Rihanna, Eva Mendes, Elizabeth Taylor, Steve Jobs, Justin Bieber, Drew Barrymore, Bruce Willis, Jon Bon Jovi

"Imagination is more important than knowledge."

Albert Einstein,
Pisces – theoretical physicist

COMPATIBLE
and
INCOMPATIBLE
SIGNS

You may have noticed that your friends and loved ones fall into two or three signs, while getting along with others can be a challenge. For instance, a logical "air sign" type, such as a Gemini, would find it hard to understand an artistic and intuitive Pisces. This chapter shows the sun signs you would most likely be compatible with as loved ones, friends or even neighbours, along with those who you would feel reasonably comfortable with in most settings. The table at the end of this chapter also points out the signs that you find difficult. It will even explain the frustrating fact that there are those who appear to get on perfectly well with people who you find utterly impossible. Please keep in mind that we are looking at basic sun sign astrology, not the fully detailed picture from a natal chart.

SIGNS
and ELEMENTS

Each sign belongs to an element of fire, earth, air or water, and the chart (see page 174) shows the system in action. Aries is the first sign, and its symbol is on the left in the nine o'clock position. Aries is a fire sign. Moving on in an anti-clockwise direction, the next symbol is Taurus, an earth sign; then you see the symbol for the air sign of Gemini, followed by the symbol for the water sign of Cancer. The system now starts again – in the same order – with the next four signs, and then repeats once more for the last group of four signs.

Those who have knowledge of astrology will realize that there are other sun-sign links due to shared planetary influences, but that is for a more advanced book than this one.

ARIES

21 march – 19 april

Aries is a fire sign, so it is compatible with the other fire signs of Leo and Sagittarius, while Arians also get on well with the air signs of Gemini, Libra and Aquarius. Libra is on the opposite side of the chart from Aries, and this combination often works very well in friendship or as lovers. The signs that are least compatible with Aries are the earth signs of Taurus, Virgo and Capricorn, and the water signs of Cancer, Scorpio and Pisces.

TAURUS

20 april – 20 may

Taurus is an earth sign, so it is compatible with the other earth signs of Virgo and Capricorn. Taureans get on well with the water signs of Cancer, Scorpio and Pisces, and they can be drawn to the sign on the opposite side of the chart, which is Scorpio. They find it far less easy to cope with the fire signs of Aries, Leo and Sagittarius, and they find the air signs of Gemini, Libra and Aquarius irritating.

GEMINI

21 may – 20 june

Gemini is an air sign, so it is compatible with the air signs of Libra and Aquarius, although Geminis also get on well with the fire sign group of Aries, Leo and Sagittarius. Sagittarius is on the opposite side of the chart to Gemini, so that can make for a very happy relationship. The difficult signs are the earth signs of Taurus, Virgo and Capricorn, and the water signs of Cancer, Scorpio and Pisces.

CANCER

21 june – 22 july

Cancer is a water sign, which gets on well with the other water signs of Scorpio and Pisces, and it is also harmonious with the earth signs of Taurus, Virgo and Capricorn. It might be comfortable with Capricorn because this is on the other side of the chart to Cancer, which makes an interesting combination. The signs that Cancer finds tricky to cope with are the fire signs of Aries, Leo and Sagittarius, and the air signs of Gemini, Libra and Aquarius.

LEO

23 july – 22 august

Leo is a fire sign, so it is especially compatible with the other fire signs of Aries and Sagittarius, but it gets on well with the air signs of Gemini, Libra and Aquarius. Leo and Aquarius are on opposite sides of the chart, which makes them an exciting and enjoyable combination. The signs that are harder for Leo to cope with are the earth signs Taurus, Virgo and Capricorn, and the water signs of Cancer, Scorpio and Pisces.

♍

VIRGO

23 august – 22 september

Virgo is an earth sign, so it works well with the earth signs of Taurus and Capricorn, and it does well with the water signs of Cancer, Scorpio and Pisces. The sign on the opposite side of the chart is Pisces, so these two could make a good partnership. The signs that irritate Virgo are the fire signs of Aries, Leo and Sagittarius, and the air signs of Gemini, Libra and Aquarius.

♎

LIBRA

23 september – 22 october

Libra is an air sign, compatible with the other air signs of Gemini and Aquarius, and it also gets on well with the fire signs of Aries, Leo and Sagittarius. Libra and Aries are on opposite sides of the chart, so they make a good combination. Less compatible signs are the earth signs of Taurus, Virgo and Capricorn and the water signs of Cancer, Scorpio and Pisces.

♏

SCORPIO

23 october – 21 november

Scorpio is a water sign, so it is comfortable with the other water signs of Cancer and Pisces, while it is friendly with the earth signs of Taurus, Virgo and Capricorn. Taurus is on the opposite side of the chart to Scorpio, which makes this couple an excellent match. The less compatible signs are the fire signs of Aries, Leo and Sagittarius, and the air signs of Gemini, Libra and Aquarius.

SAGITTARIUS

22 november – 21 december

As a fire sign, Sagittarius relates well to the other fire signs of Aries and Leo, and it gets on with the air signs of Gemini, Libra and Aquarius. Sagittarius is on the opposite side of the chart to Gemini, so that often makes a good match. It finds it hard to link with the earth signs of Taurus, Virgo and Capricorn, and the water signs of Cancer, Scorpio and Pisces.

♑

CAPRICORN

22 december – 19 january

Capricorn, an earth sign, links well with the other earth signs of Taurus and Virgo, and it is also compatible with the water signs of Cancer, Scorpio and Pisces. Capricorn is on the opposite side of the chart to Cancer, so those two often do well together. This sign finds it challenging to live with the fire signs of Aries, Leo and Sagittarius, and the air signs of Gemini, Libra or Aquarius.

AQUARIUS

20 january – 18 february

Aquarius is an air sign that combines well with the other air signs of Gemini and Libra, but also with the fire signs of Aries, Leo and Sagittarius. Aquarius and Leo are on opposite sides of the chart, so they can work well in a relationship. Aquarius finds it harder to cope with the earth signs of Taurus, Virgo and Capricorn, and the water signs of Cancer, Scorpio and Pisces.

♓

PISCES

19 february – 20 march

Pisces, a water sign, gets on well with the other water signs of Cancer and Scorpio, and the earth signs of Taurus, Virgo and Capricorn. Pisces is on the opposite side of the chart to Virgo, so that can make a successful relationship. The signs that Pisces finds hard to like are the fire signs of Aries, Leo and Sagittarius, and the air signs of Gemini, Libra and Aquarius.

compatibility chart

	AIR	TAU	GEM	CAN	LEO	VIR
AIR	★	✖	•	✖	★	✖
TAU	✖	★	✖	•	✖	★
GEM	•	✖	★	✖	•	✖
CAN	✖	•	✖	★	✖	•
LEO	★	✖	•	✖	★	✖
VIR	✖	★	✖	•	✖	★
LIB	•	✖	★	✖	•	✖
SCO	✖	•	✖	★	✖	•
SAG	★	✖	•	✖	★	✖
CAP	✖	★	✖	•	✖	★
AQU	•	✖	★	✖	•	✖
PIS	✖	•	✖	★	✖	•

see page 192 for notes

	LIB	SCO	SAG	CAP	AQU	PIS
AIR	•	✖	★	✖	•	✖
TAU	✖	•	✖	★	✖	•
GEM	★	✖	•	✖	★	✖
CAN	✖	★	✖	•	✖	★
LEO	•	✖	★	✖	•	✖
VIR	✖	•	✖	★	✖	•
LIB	★	✖	•	✖	★	✖
SCO	✖	★	✖	•	✖	★
SAG	•	✖	★	✖	•	✖
CAP	✖	•	✖	★	✖	•
AQU	★	✖	•	✖	★	✖
PIS	✖	★	✖	•	✖	★

COMPATIBILITY CHART

The chart on pages 190–191 indicates the ways that the signs relate to each other.

★ A star specifies the good matches

● A dot shows the reasonable ones

✖ The cross highlights the ones that would be a struggle